Multifaceted

KIERON BLAKE

Presentation by *BookLeaf Publishing*

Web: www.bookleafpub.com

E-mail: info@bookleafpub.com

ISBN: 9789358313192

First edition 2023

This book is dedicated to my Grandma Letey, my Auntie Yvonne and my cousins Leighanne and Sadie. Gone, but never forgotten

ACKNOWLEDGEMENT

For my sons, Jayden and Jarrell, with love and gratitude. Daddy loves you both lots xxx

PREFACE

Within these pages, you will find a collection of verses that seek to illuminate the Black British experience in all its beauty, complexity, and depth. Poetry, with its power to distill the essence of our emotions and thoughts, has long been a sanctuary for the soul, offering a glimpse into the ineffable aspects of our lives. This poetry book, like many others, invites you to embark on a journey, but its destination is a place that only you can truly discover—within the landscapes of your own heart and mind.

Each poem, like a snapshot of time, captures a moment, an emotion, or a reflection. The verses here are woven from the fabric of my experiences, from the threads of love, loss, hope, and despair. They are born from the richness of our human condition, and in their words, you may find the echoes of your own joys, aspirations, sorrows, and dreams.

Whilst the poems contained herein are shaped by the thoughts and feelings of me, they are also shaped by you, the reader. In the private theatre of your mind, these words take on new life.

They adapt to your experiences, resonating with the moments that are uniquely yours. In this collaboration between me, the writer and you, the reader, the magic of poetry truly unfolds.

As you peruse these verses, you will encounter various themes and topics—love and belonging, life's beauty, the passage of time, and the intricacies of the human heart. You may find solace in the familiar or be challenged by the unfamiliar. The beauty of poetry lies in its ability to evoke a multitude of emotions and interpretations, providing something for everyone and everybody.

This collection is an invitation to pause, reflect, and connect with your own thoughts and feelings. It is an exploration of the ineffable, a journey through the landscapes of the human spirit. I hope you find within these pages a mirror that reflects your own experiences, and a window that opens onto new perspectives.

In the words that follow, may you discover a refuge for your own musings and a companion for your own journey. For, in poetry, we are all travelers and guides, setting out on an adventure with every turn of the page. The magic of this literary form lies in its ability to bridge the gap between writer and reader, to awaken the heart, and to remind us of the infinite power of words. I thank you for joining me on this poetic voyage. I hope you find your own stories, your own emotions, and your own reflections in the verses that grace these pages.

Grandma's House

In Grandma's house, memories dwell,

Where time stands still, and stories tell.

Amongst the relics of days gone by,

I sip Baldwin's Sarsaparilla, oh so sly.

With every drop, the past unfurls,

In dark liquid, nostalgia swirls.

Her presence lingers in each old frame,

As whispers of love, like candles, flame.

The creaky floorboards echo my tread,

Through halls of yesteryears, I'm led.

Wilmers Court, Elms Court,

Holds secrets and dreams, those she wove.

As I sip the Sarsaparilla's sweet embrace,
I glimpse her smile, feel her warm embrace.

Her laughter echoes in the gentle breeze,

Through windows open, inviting ease.

In the corner, her chair stands,

A sentinel of time, holding her plans.

I close my eyes, and there she appears,

A guardian angel, calming my fears.

The scent of Sunday dinner arises,

Her culinary magic, a sweet surprise.

With Baldwin's Sarsaparilla, a perfect pair,

I relive her love and tender care.

The walls adorned with cherished art,

Masterpieces created with her heart.

Her creativity forever etched in space,

Her loving touch, no time can erase.
In this house, her spirit still roams,

A sanctuary of love, our precious home.

With each sip of sarsaparilla divine,

Her legacy lives on, her soul aligns.

As evening descends, stars light the skies,

And tears may fall from my weary eyes.

Yet, in this place, her memory's secure,

Forever cherished, her love endures.

So, I'll keep drinking Baldwin's brew,

Remembering the joy she once knew.

In Grandma's house, I'll find my way,

Guided by her love, come what may.

Double Heartbreak

Double Heartbreak

Double Heartbreak

End of a 4-year relationship left me with a broken heart, whilst getting blown out on Valentine's Day left me with a bruised and deflated ego.

Don't know what made me fall for that Teacher but there were so many lessons I wanted to teach her. Like being a good wife as opposed to being a good-time girl with a fucked up life.

Sorry for using '**' as a pawn in my game but emotionally I was violated and mentally I was humiliated. Never wear your heart on your sleeve and always keep your cards close to your chest.

Double Heartbreak

Double Heartbreak

Meanwhile, ex-wifey has moved to another
brother, as I try to reconcile with my mother.

Sent her a letter and she wasn't having a bar of
it. Wrote the Teacher a letter but never sent it. I
put it in a bottle and posted it down the river
hoping some poor sod would find it and try and
reconcile us. In retrospect I would have sent the
Teacher the letter, and not sent the letter to my
ex-wifey. Repressed feelings made me feel like
Emily Bronte starring in Villette

Double Heartbreak

Double Heartbreak

I tell ******* I'm no ping pong ball and this
isn't no rebound ting! Don't make my mistake of
letting a few months pass and jumping into the
deep end. You will only drown in your fears and
tears.

Getting my heart mash-up twice was Karma and
payback for all the women I fucked and fucked
over.

Finding out about Donna dying on the way to
Loughton was like a thorn cutting through my

back. Like Nicky and Master D, she has gone
but will be never forgotten, R.I.P.

Double Heartbreak

Double Heartbreak

Running over that girl was a reflection of my
reckless behaviour. Standing up in court for
another offence with no shame or no honour. 3
points and a reduced fine; I got a bly.

Reached out to the Teacher and still no reply.
Went to Turkey so I could dry my eyes. Months
have passed and 'we' still don't talk. Visions of
my ex-wifey reoccur and I get a lifeline.
Reached out to the ex-wifey, and she gave me
time. Talking to her eased the pain like salt and
vinegar heals a wound.

A sense of closure gained and resolution
complete? 'We' still haven't crossed paths but
I'm sure we will meet. The two Gorgeous'
you've been at, I never got in or I was meant to
go but didn't.

Man dem tell me they have seen 'you' and I
wanna sing 'tell me have you seen her'. Sly
subconscious kicking in. Got a good woman in

****** and a 'substitute' on the sideline in
******.

My eyes well up but the tears can't come. I
haven't mourned for Donna and I can't 'mourn'
for you two either. For the time being, my
feelings need to take a breather…

I pause. I wonder what to write down next. I
only know pain, sorrow, bitterness, resentment,
jealousy, envy, hurt and wounded pride

In hindsight, the two of 'unoo' weren't meant for
me or else I wouldn't be doing this…

Double Heartbreak

Double Heartbreak

Zoot

In a world of smoke, I find my way,

A zoot, a flame, where thoughts sway.

No needles, no powders, just nature's grace,

I light the fire, in a tranquil space.

I don't smoke for highs that fly,

But to steady the storm when life gets high.

No powders to blind, no needles to inject,

Just a soothing burn, a moment to introspect.

A zoot is my compass, my guide through the
mist,

A chance to ponder, to reminisce.

In its gentle embers, my worries dissolve,

A chance to connect, my problems resolved.

So I'll bun a zoot, let the worries take flight,

Watch the curling smoke in the soft moonlight.

With each whispered exhale, a burden unchains,

In the fragrant dance, a mindful refrain.

No injecting desires, no snorting away,

Just a zoot to keep the chaos at bay.

I'll continue to reflect, as the embers burn slow,

In this tranquil ritual, my mind finds its flow.

Death

In London's shadowed streets, you'd think I'd see
my first encounter with death's decree.

But no, in Brussels' heart, it came to be,

A scene from a dark gangster's spree.

Po-Po raced in their whips, lights ablaze,

Chaos unfolded in a bewildering haze.

People scattered like frenzied birds,

In the midst of it all, the truth unfurled.

A body, limp and torn, met my eyes,

A horrifying sight beneath sorrowful skies.

His van askew, like a twisted bangle,

Life's fragile thread caught in fate's tangle.

Shattered glass adorned the ground,

Bullet holes etched a tragic sound.

Amidst the chaos, a crowd amassed,

Witnessing a moment that forever would last.

This scene of anguish, so hard to bear,

A testament to a world unfair.

In the heart of a city, so much despair,

A reminder that life is fragile, handled with care.

From London's alleys to Brussels' squares,

Tragedy strikes, and no one spares.

The pain that ripples through every soul,

As violence and chaos take their toll.

But in the midst of darkness, we must unite,

To seek a future where justice takes flight.

For though this world can be unjust and cruel,

Together, we can work to mend and rule.

She

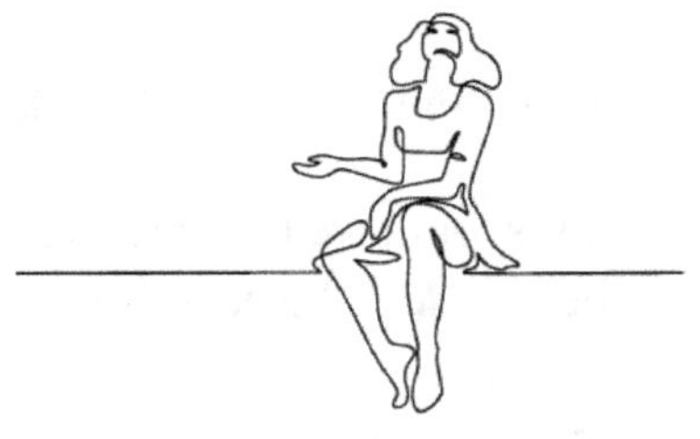

She, a tapestry of dreams untold,

In her presence, a story unfolds.

A twist of fate, an unexpected delight,

A journey together, taking flight.

Never thought this would happen, I admit,

Yet destiny wove our paths to fit.

Asking myself how things could be,

A question that echoes, captivating me.

Taking steps towards a future unknown,

In your company, I've truly grown.

To a next level, we dare to tread,

A world of possibilities lies ahead.

Asking myself, should we be more than friends,
Lovers, partners, where the heart transcends?

A couple formed by fate's decree,

In your eyes, a world of wonders I see.

For You, I'd traverse mountains high,

Underneath the star-studded sky.

Everlasting, a promise in each heartbeat,

You and Me, in harmony complete.

A story of 'us' written in the stars,

Bound by love that forever chars.

Side by side, through life's vast sea,

Everlasting, You and Me, meant to be.

I Hate You

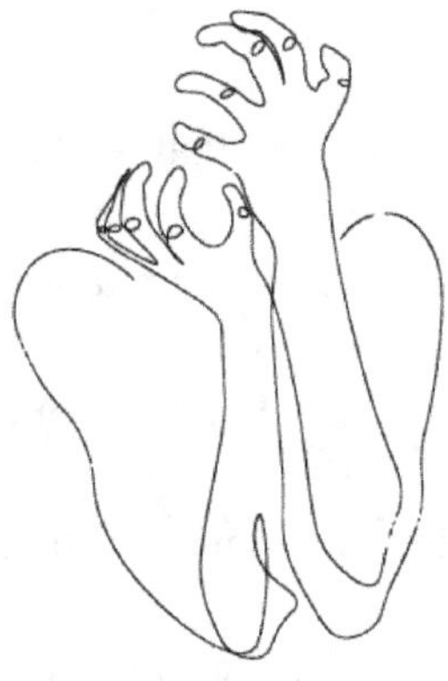

Rags, I'm putting thoughts to paper,

These feelings are raw, I can't defer or taper.

This can't wait till later, it's time to explore,

The whirlwind of emotions that churn at my
core.

What the fuck is happening with me and you?

Seven months together, yet our bond's askew.

Fuss and fight, our constant theme,

***** or *****, it's a relentless stream.

Oversensitivity lurking in the fray,

I admit, it's my demons that lead the way.

Arguments stem from my untamed soul,

In this sea of discord, I've lost control.

I pen these words in a quiet hurting,

Sleep eludes me, emotions churning.

Have we exhausted our shared course?

Or should we have lingered as friends, not worse?

A ticket abroad, an escape so keen,

From this stress, this aggro, this strife unforeseen.

Once so close, I question if I've let you too near,

Yet as friends, our worlds were simpler, clear.

I've hidden beneath a veneer so tough,

Lied about ugliness, I admit, it's rough.

You see through my masks, the real me
unveiled,

And I'm struggling to face the truths unveiled.

Arguments tear at my heart's fragile core,

I long for peace, for conflict no more.

Have we reached our end, our final course?

You mean so much, a connection I can't divorce.

But this turmoil within is tearing me apart,

A storm of emotions, a broken heart.

The dissertation, a metaphor for life's weight,

A burden to succeed, to stave off fate.

Back to us, I'm willing to fight,

Lay down the law, make everything right.

A me and you that defies the fray,

A path to rediscover, a brighter day.

These feelings echo, demanding a change,

In the script of our lives, a rearrange.

I want there to be an 'us,' I must confess,

But transformation is key, our love to address.

I love you

********, my friend, my lover, my partner true,

Grateful for all you've done, all we've been through.

Pictures of you and me, a tapestry of memories,

Hoping for more, avoiding life's thorned inquiries.

Proud to call you mine, my beautiful girl,

Intelligent and understanding, a rare pearl.

You've got your head screwed on, a solid stand,

Not lost in superficial, materialistic sand.

I need you beside me, a constant embrace,

In your absence, I yearn for your trace.

Your scent on the pillow, a lingering sweet,

Tears of longing, our hearts' silent beat.
When we intertwine, souls unite in flight,

Sharing parts of ourselves, woven so tight.

Soul-ties that bridge the realms of existence,

Physical, emotional, a love with no distance.

Like Outkast's melody, "I'm in love again," I say,

No, it's deeper, truer, in every way.

What we share, no one else can possess,

A connection that defies chaos and stress.

Special and tender, our love's gentle flow,

No wild benders, no tumultuous woe.

To hold you, not to change, my desire,

For you're a blazing star, my heart's eternal fire.

You are your own person, a light so bright,

I cherish you as you are, day and night.

You understand my ways, my heart you unfold,
A love story written in letters of gold.

I've got profound love, 'pure' in every way,

A commitment that forever will stay.

Lines may be short, but love stands tall,

****** *****, my everything, my all.

Amidst a sea of others, you stand true,

In a world of fakery, I choose you.

Only one woman ignites my soul's view,

And that woman, my love, is none but you.

Repression

Listen closely, for I have words to share,

A truth to unveil, a weight to bear.

That time you entered my realm, it was
profound,

Deeper than I imagined, a connection unbound.

Never thought we'd traverse such depths,

Two souls intertwined, like secrets kept.

Low, dependent, yet seeking more,

Rags, you ignited a yearning core.

Your problems, your tales, mirrored mine,

A reflection in your eyes, so divine.

When our lips met, a long-held desire,

Flames of passion rising higher and higher.

The chemistry between us, an intense flame,

Desires unspoken, with no one to blame.

That night, perhaps it was meant to be,

But destiny played a different melody.

I know you sought more than a fleeting tide,

I fell for you, emotions I couldn't hide.

Seeing you hurt, crying for the wrong,

It pierces me, a pain so strong.

Together, we'd be a force to embrace,

But 'family' you say, a term we must face.

Wishing for more, while you stand fast,

An opportunity missed, a chance gone past.

I'd make you my queen, if given the chance,

A life together, a true romance.

But buried deep, emotions I'll hide,
Like the woman in Villette, I'll abide.

Your tears, your joy, I feel them too,

Linked in this journey, me and you.

The truth stark and clear, a tale so sad,

You've moved forward, while I'm left feeling
mad.

Let's leave it here, as painful as it sounds,

You've moved on, while my heart still drowns.

Listen, my words confess the truth we face,

You've healed, while I'm caught in love's
embrace.

Paranoia

What the fuck is happening to me?

Once carefree, now I'm lost at sea.

From that joyful Black guy, I've turned,

Into a saddened soul, lessons hard-earned.

I search for the moment where it went awry,

In Belgium, perhaps, or when London's sky,

Enveloped me in shadows, dark and cold,

Depression's grip, a story to be told.

I yearn for the end, this ceaseless plight,

Hating the darkness that shrouds my light.

A pendulum of emotions, swinging wild,

One day up, the next, I'm defiled.

I'm well aware of the truth within,
Depressed, a battle I'm trying to win.

Antidepressant path I won't tread,

Mood swings tormenting, filling me with dread.

Furious rages flare like a storm,

A desire to hurt, to cause harm.

But it's not what they think, not schizophrenia's
dance,

I won't be locked away, a twisted circumstance.

Blazing weed, a futile solace it seems,

A journey far from my peaceful dreams.

Uni brought change, a path I'll reverse,

Leaving as I came, this habit dispersed.

Kieron's name carries weight, can't falter or slip,

Pressure immense, failure's grip.

But I see the future, bright and clear,

Big tings ah gwarn, no room for fear.

Time ticks away, each moment a call,

Tick tock, I rise, I won't let it fall.

Though lines may be short, these words resound,

Change will come, happiness unbound.

Mark my words, I declare with might,

Gee, things will shift, once more the light.

Though battles remain, strength will break
through,

I will be happy again, my pledge to you.

Typical day in Brussels/I wrote this one in Brussels

Today feels like a heavy weight,

Shitty emotions, no love to sate.

Woke up to silence, a barren screen,

Isolation's grip, a lonely scene.

Saturday's memory, a bitter taste,

*****, unkindness laid to waste.

Words that hurt, attacks unkind,

Sadness swirling in my mind.

Through the station, a choked-up air,

As if tears long suppressed lay bare.

Pain au Fromage, a flavourless bite,

Replay, The Sun, out of sight.

Late train woes, frustrations swell,

The world's injustices, a tale to tell.

Taxi man's bias, a needless fight,

Raging thoughts, emotions ignite.

Training drags, a mundane score,

Cigarette craving, seeking more.

Salad's call, a choice to mend,

New shirt's hope, a path to wend.

Lost and empty, emotions collide,

Fatigue engulfs, nowhere to hide.

Messages absent, popularity fades,

Boredom bites, as Madman KILO invades.

Channelling energy, a need to release,

Yearning to kick a ball, find inner peace.

The trainer senses, something's amiss,
Lost in thoughts, an emotional abyss.

Writing thoughts, a therapy's grace,

Chi's ebbing flow, a mindful space.

Lethargy's clasp, exhaustion's toll,

Coca Cola's craving, a thirst to console.

Missed connections, *****, on my mind,

Needy or not, a balance to find.

Yet I remember, I was whole before,

Drake's anthem echoes, confidence's roar.

Aching head, a French lament,

New shirt's quest, a goal intent.

*****'s wants, a mystery to decode,

Eyes closing, to dream's abode.

In slumber's embrace, a wish takes flight,

To be like *******, a beacon of light.
Through the ups and downs, emotions sway,

This day's journey, in words, I convey.

******: Part 2

In a tale that's woven through time's thread,

Where memories dance, a story widespread,

I struggle to find where to commence,

Remembering moments that left their imprints
dense.

First meeting etched in my mind so clear,

A phone shop encounter, destiny's frontier.

A One2One connection, a leap so bold,

Your beauty, your essence, my heart took hold.

Coolie skin that stirred my desires,

Long hair flowing, stoking love's fires.

Breasts that beckoned, hips and thighs,

A desire to caress, under moonlit skies.

Our first date, a dance of fate,

Desire's flame burned, a longing to sate.

Titties tasted, a passion's tease,

Hayes for a meal, a moment to please.

I remember those times, the highs and the lows,

A rollercoaster journey where love ebbed and
rose.

Summer's madness, a storm in the air,

Contributed to our downfall, love's affair.

Then came the moment, two bodies entwined,

"Bare back" you declared, but my mind
declined.

Sex that sizzled, our bodies' symphony,

Ragga and Dancehall, our rhythm's harmony.

Valentine's deep, candles' soft glow,

Presents, cards, and strawberry yogurt's flow.
But shadows loomed, struggles took hold,

Jobs lost, realities escaped and untold.

Arguments brewed, a stormy sea,

Right and wrong clashed, a battle for glee.

The violence that once broke through,

Darkened the skies, love's crimson hue.

Broken windows, a bathroom's despair,

Fatty shouts in the air.

Our love's tale faltered, fractured in strife,

A village bike's whispers, a bittersweet life.

Seeing you anew, a mirror of the past,

A reminder that love's death can't be recast.

Issues unaddressed, the past still haunting,

Two paths diverged, heartache and wanting.

Our paths have parted, as destinies sway,
Your journey, your own, mine in the day.

May you find solace, redemption's embrace,

A chance to heal, and your inner storms erase.

Case of the ex

A year passed by, silence's embrace,

Then you resurface, a familiar face.

Wanting to meet, to converse anew,

Despite past wrongs, a bridge to construe.

Naturally skeptical, I tread with care,

Your intentions hidden, a truth to bear.

Setting traps, your motives shrouded,

N****s in tow, intentions clouded.

But I'm not naive, not easily led,

Connections in your world, secrets spread.

Numbers on speed dial, allies close,

Kilo, the Journeyman, knowledge he bestows.

London's map, etched in his mind,

Navigating alleys, the streets he'll find.

No 'whip' required, his steps assured,

No blips deter, his presence secured.

A chessboard of shadows, a game of wits,

I navigate wisely, in life's complex fits.

A meeting's offer, a twist in the plot,

Through cunning and foresight, I'll claim my shot.

Promiscuity

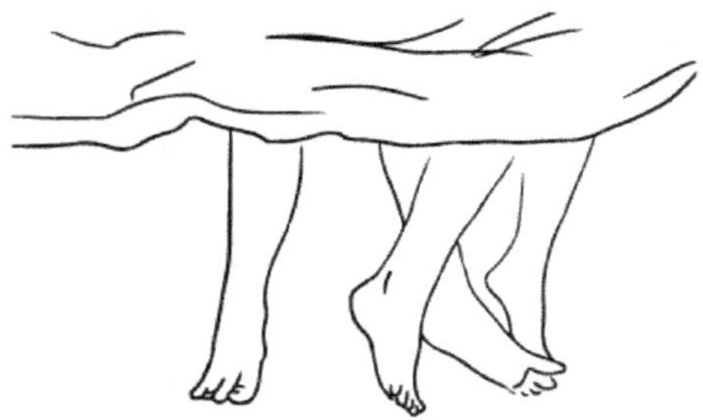

In shadows' grip, my self-esteem wanes,

Cheating's path, driven by inner pains.

I undervalue my worth, my soul's esteem,

Perfect wifey beside, yet I chase a distant dream.

Seeking grimey chicks, low desires entwine,

Three times, they're mine, lust's design.

Barebacking through recklessness, I fall,

Lax in judgment, heedless call.

Father's footsteps echoing in my stride,

Two women, two worlds, my life's divide.

A son in tow, a complex blend,

Blessed and stressed, life's story penned.

Happiness and vexation intertwine,
One life's joys, another's confines.

All this turmoil, a tale untold,

A ***** who couldn't keep his lust controlled.

Illicit deeds, a path gone astray,

Dark choices made, light kept at bay.

Unwholesome actions, taint on the soul,

In another man's corner, a role played foul.

As the sun sets on these darkened trails,

Lessons learned, and truth prevails.

A journey forward, a chance to amend,

To heal and grow, as old paths we transcend.

Why?

In 2001, our paths first crossed,

A journey that was bound, but soon exhausted.

By 2003, we reached the end,

Yet in 2005, your voice still sends.

Calling my name, echoes from the past,

Questions linger, reasons to amass.

You turned your mother's heart against me,

Painted tales of pain and cruelty.

A chick-beater, a two-timing tale,

Innocence lost, trust did fail.

In anger's grip, thoughts turned fierce,

Two shots to fate, decisions pierced.

You gave me blues, though you hid the truth,

Bruises unseen, concealed in youth.

Secrets held, air tinged with hue,

A web of lies, emotions askew.

And if your man knew of your deceit,

Truth's eruption, air's defeat.

Questions rise, the sky turns blue,

Choices to make, a life renewed.

Quantum of Solace

I can see things are changing by the way people
are behaving.
Every day I see someone reading scripture, like
it was a permanent fixture,
Words and wisdom are the mixture, Jehovah
Witness claiming GOD can fix ya'.
I bruise and I blister
Can you tell my ex I still really miss her.
Nothing lasts forever and the apple never falls
far from the tree.
I'll be killing them softly like Lauren, as I try to
get to the top of the hill.
As a child, you will told Allah reigns supreme
I was told Jesus was my saviour.
He can fix things like Dr Octavia.

But Jesus didn't have 4 hands like Shiva and he
definitely wasn't licking out beaver or smoking
purple haze cannabis sativa.
King Solomon was full of knowledge and
wisdom, and I'm on fucking out chicks in
Lisbon.
I read Psalms before I go to bed, as tomorrow is
never promised.
Tonight was the night I can say I truly found
peace and my quantum of solace.

Carnival

When Carnival arrives, a chaotic scene,
Guys on the prowl, two things in between,
Beef and chicks, an eternal dance,
A twisted tango, fuelled by chance.

Chicks and beef, a dual obsession,
Their minds consumed, no time for discretion.
Desire elusive, a fickle game they play,
Yearning for more, every single day.

It's irony's jest, this dance of fate,
When wanted, it hides, makes them wait.
When undesired, it leaps to the fore,
A cruel twist, life's relentless chore.

Guys grasping for shanks, for phones, for might,
For power, control, to win the fight.
Straps and doms, they clutch in hand,
A desperate bid to command life's sand.

Girls caught in a web, doggied, ensnared,
In this whirlwind, they're often impaired.
Jaws break, fists collide, chaos and war,
A cycle of violence, forevermore.

Foot to the floor, the tempo doesn't slow,
Desire's hunger, a persistent undertow.
He craves for arms, for pleasure's delight,
When denied, vexation takes its flight.

Carnival's wild rhythm, a tale untold,
Where desires run rampant, bold and cold.
Beef and chicks, their consuming fire,
A dance that never ceases, desire's dire.

When Carnival fades, the dust will clear,
But the echoes of passion will still adhere.
Two things dominate the fervent quest,
Beef and chicks, in a world so obsessed.

Black and British 2004

Oh my, the year is 2004,
Places where raw wounds still pour.
For a Black man to walk, to tread with care,
In a world where prejudices still ensnare.

White men's slurs, like poisoned dart,
Cussing, booing, aiming to tear apart.
"N****r," they hiss, with a snide little grin,
"Darkie" they taunt, as wars begin.

Bush in Iraq, devastation and pain,
Labels like "coon," a hurtful disdain.
Acting white like the moon, they jeer and mock,
As I stand proud, like granite rock.

So I pose the question, loud and clear,
Is being Black and British not worthy, not dear?
Would you have me leave, back to the past?
To colonies and struggles, leaving shadows cast?

Is it fear of me taking your woman's heart?
Or fear of me tearing worlds apart?
Scared of property, through Mugabe's stance,
Reclaims land in a power dance.

I want everyone to see,
I can't roam free, carelessly, to.
Bermondsey, Cheshunt, Eltham, and more,
Scuffles in Feltham, a bitter score.

All because of my skin, my heritage,
Black and British, a life's collage.
Challenges we face, yet rise we do,
Strong and proud, our spirits renew.

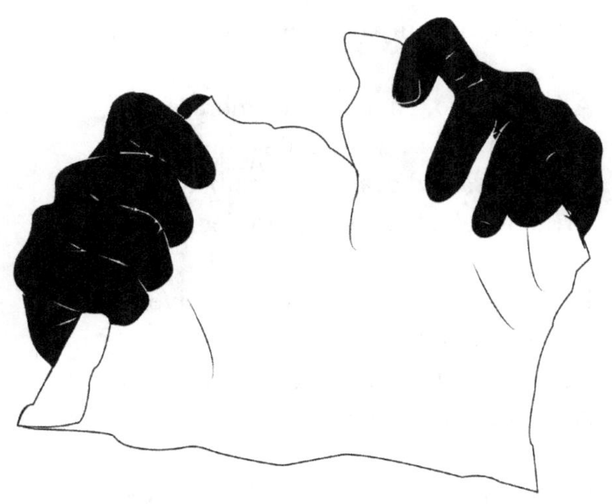

Life Part 2

Controversy's shadow dances 'round my name,
Raw, outspoken, blunt, I stake my claim.
To those who despise, I say it clear,
If I'm not your cup, then fuck off from here.

Taken for a fool, one time too much,
I've learned, grown wise, I've got that touch.
No longer a rug, no one's stepping stone,
I stand strong, my independence shown.

A lick or two, I'm ready to embrace,
Giving hits if needed, in this life's chase.
Times I wanted death, tears unbidden,
Cries of pain, but still I've ridden.

Hustling through days just to survive,
21 years, a rollercoaster ride.
Achievements vast, yet my tears remain,
A private sea, a hidden strain.

Deepest fears faced, in shadows walked,
Actions taken, some have talked.
Detrimental choices, paths I tread,
Controversy's child, where lines are thread.

Suicidal whispers, darkest hour,
Gratitude to God, to a higher power.
Not wholly bad, nor all that's good,
In shades of gray, I've often stood.

Misunderstood, a label I wear,
A complex heart, a soul laid bare.
Controversy's child, a journey's cost,
Through trials and triumphs, my life is
embossed.

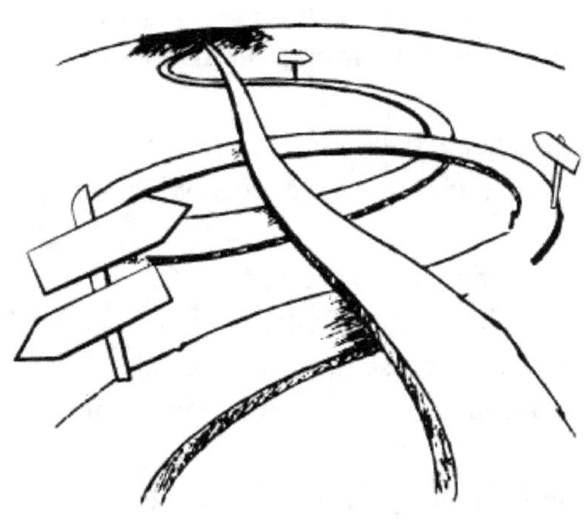

*****, Part 1

I remember days of old, a love once true,
You, my wifey, I, your man through and
through.
Kisses exchanged, caresses so divine,
Memories linger, like aged, aged wine.

Doggy styling, passions intertwined,
Moments cherished, now far behind.
Oh, girl, I miss those times we shared,
A love once bloomed, a connection so rare.

But winds of change swept in, my dear,
Love's landscape altered, crystal clear.
I admit my faults, played the fool's part,
Yet you, too, played a role, tearing at my heart.

Acting like a bitch, words you hurled,
When truth be told, your mouth didn't swirl.
The pain, it grew, like an ache inside,
Unseen battles waged, hearts torn wide.

Never intended harm, but life's course is strange,
We tried to heal, but things were rearranged.
Our first kiss, a lyrical embrace,
First war, wounds carved upon our face.
No intentions to hurt, yet pain took hold,
Love's journey's story, sometimes bold.
When I soared high, you descended low,
Vice versa played, life's ever-changing flow.

Wrong turns were made, a relationship's cost,
A bond now shattered, lost in the frost.
I hold no blame, for you played your part,
Shame you brought, tearing at my heart.

Your pain ran deep, wrists in despair,
Sectioned thoughts floated through the air.
Windows shattered, a storm within,
You needed help, love's fray so thin.

Now you've moved on, new chapters turn,
Yet echoes whisper, your love still yearns.
For deep within your heart, I see,
Remnants linger, the love for me.

Soaps

Young and restless, my spirit untamed,
Bold and beautiful, in life's game I'm named.
Family Affairs I've faced, a story to unfold,
Countless days ahead, tales yet untold.

No Cockney accent, I'm no Eastender true,
'Bare fuckery' I speak, pretense I eschew.
A 'northern lass' by my side, a Corrie soul,
Spain's Eldorado she seeks, with Emma and
Dale.

One day, my dynasty will rise to the sky,
Oil's kingpin, like JR in Dallas, I'll fly.
Though knots and tangles my path may entwine,
If I stumble, I hope for a landing divine.

Life's journey ahead, an open road to explore,
A canvas for stories, mysteries galore.
Youth's vigor and fire, my heart shall defend,
Bold and beautiful, my tale won't end.

Frustration

Amidst the frustration, people seek change's call,
Life's trials push them, make them rise and fall.
MCs transform to rappers, fueled by inner fire,
Girls frustrated, become slappers, but their
dreams never tire.

Geeks turn dapper, male kidnappers in despair,
Yet their journeys lead to crossroads where they
stare.
The hype's brief thrill fades like twilight's song,
Revealing lost souls, yearning to belong.

I ponder the questions that echo in my mind,
A paradox of dreams that's hard to unwind.
Rocking Avirex, no whip to my name,
Chasing desires, yet it's not the same.

Wooing a girl, but with no dom on my side,

Locked car, no key, a challenging ride.
Towards my aspirations, I strive to sprint,
To the place where my heart and dreams are
intently meant.

From MC to artist, a transformation bold,
Like a pyromaniac from flames untold.
Like a weed smoker seeking solace anew,
A reporter's voice to journalism is so true.

I'll forge that shift, embrace the change,
Within my range, a journey to arrange.
Life's cycle spins like a washing drum's dance,
A rollercoaster ride, fate's wild chance.

A jigsaw puzzle of pieces scattered wide,
In patience and effort, their places abide.
These lyrics from Brussels, a city's embrace,
Not London's scene, a different space.

Penned in a haze, thoughts unchained and free,
Tequila, Duvel, Tripel Westmalle's glee.
In highs and twists, these words unfurled,
Desires entwined, a complex world.

From frustrations born, a creative flight,
A poet's journey, seeking the light.
Through ups and downs, a puzzle's grace,
I carve my path in life's sprawling maze.